"Oh, were every book a gift . . ."

To:

From:

Praise for *A Child's Christmas in Brooklyn*

In the literary tradition of Charles Dickens' England and Dylan Thomas' Wales . . . Frank Crocitto joins the notables.

The Roanoke Times

I admire the sense of humor, the subtlety of the reminiscences and the sheer lyricism of the treatment. A jewel, indeed.

Joseph Tusiani - Poet and translator

Recalling the family gatherings Frank's stories evoked brought back many warm memories and also made my stomach growl. Arancini & spedini! Stories like this need to be told!

Michael Badalucco - Actor

A just-long-enough visit to a place that once was.

Winston–Salem Journal

Praise for *A Child's Christmas in Brooklyn*

Ah, Christmas in Brooklyn! I felt like I was revisiting my own childhood. Frank writes from his heart to your heart! Good for me!!!

Dom DeLuise - Actor, comedian, and chef

Frank Crocitto has a masterpiece in this book as he recounts his childhood Christmases growing up. I predict this book will find itself on the Silver Screen. If done right, it will be the next classic that a cable channel will show for 24 hours at Christmas.

Bookideas.com

A wonderful memoir of growing up in Brooklyn in the 1940s—marvelous reading for any Christmas season and a delight for anytime of the year.

Reviewer's Bookwatch

A Child's Christmas in Brooklyn

A Child's Christmas in Brooklyn

Frank Crocitto

illustrations

Grady Kane-Horrigan

CANDLEPOWER

NEW PALTZ, NY

A Child's Christmas in Brooklyn.

Second Edition Revised

© 2002 Frank Crocitto

Design by David Perry & Frank Crocitto

Published by Candlepower
New Paltz, NY

ISBN 1-932037-00-4

for my father

Nicola Santa Crocitto

Season's Greetings

Nothing holds a candle to Christmas, not summertime, not Coney Island, not even Superman, Wonder Woman and the Lone Ranger all chasing the same crook. I keep the tree with its happy lights up almost to the brink of spring, and I have a Christmas cup that I drink my coffee out of all year long.

So when I wanted to give some friends a gift from my heart, I had no choice but to write them a story about Christmas. It took a while, but I did it. I called it *A Child's Christmas in Brooklyn,* though it's not a children's book, but a book for adults.

And you don't have to be from Brooklyn to enjoy it either. Actually, you just have to be grown up enough to treasure that amazing time when we saw the world as a place of beauty and wonder.

The friends I gave it to liked it so much they urged me to pass it on to you. It's a gift book—my gift to you, too. Merry Christmas.

—The Author

Christmas
came inching down the calendar
like a pasty-faced apparition,
tentative at first as syrup off a spoon,
becoming robust and ruddy-faced
as summer ripened into autumn,
promising evermore fabulous things
as the days, gathering momentum,
dipped deeper into the barrel
of December darkness;
and always, if my memory serves,
he came muffled in a swirl
of breathtaking flakes.

Oh

how

white

how

wished for

how

welcome

were

the snows

in those

days.

We held our arms out to it.
We held out our tongues for it
like we did for the Host
and when it touched
we melted with it
into ecstasy.

The more boulders
the more cliffs
and mountains that came

avalanching out of the clouds
the more deliriously wild
and wooly we became.

Snow

came
smothering the gardens,
burying the johnnypumps
up to their necks,
blurring the fencelines
and hedges
that separated
our houses.

The big snows put the kibosh on grown-ups
and their misbegotten schemes.
Their cars and trucks,
their snarling traffic—bound for nowhere—
all expired before the blade
of victorious white.

We had the streets to ourselves!

And we made good use of them, too—
pushing and shoveling up hillocks of snow,
waging great snowball wars,
tumbling and tossing and sliding,
sledding down the length of the block,
rollicking
in the stupendous,
unbounded,
elemental
whiteness.

Snow, silent,
sacred snow,
snow, the irrepressible snow,
was the herald and hymn
of Christmas coming,

and we, the boys of 81st Street, began bending our eyes Christmasward early, me especially, very early, earlier than most, setting my heart on that horizon as soon as I was done counting the booty from my birthday in July.

Birthdays are good days—good enough days—but birthdays are come-and-go days that leave us still closed in our own closet. I longed for Christmas—the great day—which held everyone, warm and one, in its wide arms. Though I knew there were forces afoot intent on destroying the joy of the approaching day.

The journey from July to the jolly, glittering tree—as long as summers were short—turned to an excruciating *via dolorosa* in the dying days of November under the yoke of extra homework and the press of projects our gnarled and sadistic schoolmarms pressed upon our hapless backs.

As our holidays drew nigh,
they delivered their ultimate, unholy,
blood-dripping threat.

> "There may have to be as-sign-ments
> over the vacation, children."

We'd been so *lackadaisical,*
I'll have you know, we *dawdled* so,
and were so often *tardy* and *untidy.*
But mostly we had persisted so
in mimicking the category of noise
that empty barrels make so superbly.
What a pity the jargon and chalkdust
of public school was never buried
with the musty bones
of Mabel E. Piercy,
our long-legged,
quavering-voiced principal,
and Miss Harbison, The Harpy,
and Mrs. O'Melia,
who rapped out the elements of arithmetic
on the cold, cold blackboard
with bare knuckles,

and Mrs. Monroe,
who could freeze the blood
in boys' veins at a hundred yards,
and Mrs. Alexander,
whose regal backside
attained fame
in song and story
due to its uncanny resemblance to a Scandinavian ski slope.

    But even *they* could not kill Christmas—not that whole dastardly coven, not with all their textbooks and tests and compositions and all their frumping and grinding, scolding, scowling—and they could not stop it either, and I knew it was breathing sweetly down our necks when Grandpa began rummaging for his Christmas lights.

Grandpa's lights were not the tree lights but the "outside-a lights" that we strung in great, looping garlands to garnish the street-side of our house—1360 - 81st Street—festooning the windows with them and the front door and the mulberry tree in the front yard. When the Lomanginos, our relatives on one side of the alley, and the Tarullis, our relatives on the other, and the scattered Panzas and Moreas and Cirillos heard Grandpa was hanging out his lights, they got cracking on theirs.

I happened to hear him rustling and humming to himself in the tool room next to the wine cellar, that wondrous wine cellar with the wainscot door which had a porthole to peep in, and space at the sill for the mixed scents of garlic braids, the lusty savor of my grandfather's wine and my grandmother's glorious hoard of tomato sauce to go wafting out into the wide world. With the care he brought to handling eggs, Grandpa was shifting the boxes of lights off the back of the big white whale of an oil tank.

My grandfather rarely took the initiative. My grandmother took so much of it there wasn't a whole lot left over. But he got Christmas going, and the vegetable garden in the spring, and the wine making and tomato canning in the fall, as well as the game of Lotto that was his personal topping to Christmas Day.

Ho, Gramps was moving like a fullback now—head low, shoulder thrown forward—and I was right behind him.

"Grandpa . . ."

"Che voo, Frangeesk?" he asked, in his sing-song, wheedling Barese dialect.

The Barese are an unsung, endearingly peculiar species of Eyetalian, springing from low-down around the ankle of "The Boot," renowned for their gullet-scraping wine, their olive oil, and their incorrigible predilection for horse meat. Alas, all the horses have vanished from the whinnying meadows of Brooklyn and our Barese heritage has suffered greatly thereby.

"Let me help, Grandpa."

"So, you wanna help-a me, huh, my little-a, big-a strong boy, Frangeesk?" Grandpa kept his stale, unlit stogy clenched between his big, bright, horse-like teeth and never looked at me.

"I can, Gramps. Can't I?" I whined, and I scuffled my feet like I had to pee. "I helped you last year. Remember, Grandpa?" I waited, hoping beyond hope.

"Alright-a," he sang, with a reluctant lilt.

Grandpa had a face round as a honeydew. The few hairs he had left—kept in place with ivory soap—were combed neatly across his grand bald head. He smiled a mischievous smile and beckoned me, "Veena daow." (which means: Come over here.)

So I sprang to his side and he delivered some cardboard boxes into my outstretched arms with the word of caution that still echoes through the haste and spume of my life:

"*Guarda,* Frangeesk, guarda!" (meaning: Watch what you're doing, Frankie!)

Grandpa and I set ourselves up in the vast

basement room—where my mother's piano was and the wind-up victrola and the large banquet table—the room where our whole family laughed, danced, argued and chomped its way through all our tumultuous holiday feasts.

Enthroned in his favorite armchair, surrounded by a tangle of green wires, he looked like a Buddha delivering a gentle lesson to a schoolful of snakes. Patiently, while extricating each string of lights from the snag, he explained to me that though he wound up each string and set them to sleep "nice-a-nice" at the end of the season, they had been "loose-a" in their boxes all year with no one to watch them, so they had twisted into "troub-la."

Then he'd wink archly, and his belly, which was the size of a bushel basket, began to vibrate gleefully. It was the same inexplicable parable year after year.

The disentangling and the re-entangling and the methodical bulb-testing took endless hours, but when all the lights were in working order we bore them like holy relics to the front of the house, and laboriously—which was my grandfather's pace—we brought the colors of the season in—first on the block!

Usually, near the climax of our heroic drive to fling a fistful of brightness into the face of a dingy world, my grandmother would come sailing out.

"Whadda we need with these stupid lights?" she'd grouch operatically.

Grandma's English was far from broken; she had gone to night school and become the mouthpiece for the family, in-season and out.

"Go back-a inside," Grandpa growled from the top of the ladder, "before you catch-a you cold."

"I never catch nothing," she scoffed majestically. "But *you*, jedrool, (which means cucumber) you're looking to make Frankie sick out here."

Grandma, bless her machinating heart, was always worried about me getting sick, which no doubt helped me to get sick as much as I did.

"Seenda-mai, Frangeesk!" Grandpa reached down and grabbed my arm with his iceman's vice-grip. "Listen to me, I need-a you help. I need-a his-a help-pa!" Grandpa proclaimed with rumbling finality.

Grandma stood there a moment, holding her ancient, buttonless mold-green sweater tightly clasped, like a miserable peasant on a wind-swept heath.

Then with a magniloquent swish of the back of her hand, her characteristic gesture of disgust, she went off grumbling something about how thestupidpoorpeople are the ones who have to make the electric company rich themiserabledogs don't steal enough money from us so we have to lightupthewholeworld so we can workourfingerstothebone to make more money so the electric company canbeeven*more*rich!

Before vanishing she would throw her eyes up to the grey, indifferent skies and send some inscrutable word or two—heavenward—into the ears of the Madonna.

Yet my Grandma liked the lights, no matter what she said. Grandpa knew that, and so did I.

Moreover the lights were a signal to Grandma, in her apartment downstairs, to Aunt Grace on the first floor, and to my mother on the floor above, to tie their aprons on and get the wheels of Christmas rolling!

O nce Grandma succumbed
to the bright-nosed cosmic fact
that Christmas was upon us,
she began a musical clattering in her
basement kitchen,
and before the day was out
she had conjured up some ineffable delight
whose essence rose in a graceful fragrance,
out and up from her warm
green-and-white stove,
up the steps,
curling up to the first floor,
rounding the bend in the front hall,
and floating up the next staircase,

melanzane alla parmigiana jewish

struffoli torta di ricotta

zeppole pane di spagna

panettone rum baba

squash soup

calamari neapolitan

...cini di ricotta scampi polen... ...bread cassata caponata savoiardi pignoli polpettone spedini gamberi con riso onion pie ingartadette

melting hearts as it climbed,
up, up, until it reached
"the upstairs"—where we lived—
and for all I know
it soared right out the skylight
away and beyond
up into the nostrils of God.

And I know he was pleased.

He had no choice.

S o Christmas was a-coming,
   a slow chug at first,
     then picking up steam,
       until—at long last—
         the whistle blew!
           We were free!!

The doors of P.S. 201 slapped open and we rampaged into the brisk, carefree air, like Mongolian hordes.

Across 12th Avenue, heedless of cars, down 81st Street, running up and along unfenced lawns, across the trolley tracks on 13th Avenue, heedless of trolleys, too.

When we reached our block, we flung our books onto the stoops and broke into the ecstatic mayhem of a snowball fight, or if there was no snow yet, it was tag, kick-the-can, johnny-on-the-pony (also known as buck-buck) or caught-caught-ringaleevio!

We were unleashed upon an unsuspecting world and we played—unsupervised in those days—creating our own games, our own rules, our own justice—scrambling till we sweat like summer under our mackinaws and had to peel them off; off flew our caps, too.

We couldn't stop even when the tides of twilight swamped us, nor even—in the undeniable dark—at that mystical moment, when all the streetlights came on at once . . .

Ah

we stopped only
when raspy maternal voices
bellowed the call to supper—
which call could not be lightly ignored.

So, exasperated by the way of a world that
permits the trivial to trample down
the essential, we shambled
grumpily
home.

Listen, listen—

I can still hear a voice—

is it Louie's, or Vinnie's or Steve's or Paulie's

or Bobby's—?

"Hey, you guys, I bettcha it's gonna *snow* tomorrow!"

A hopeful word hurled into the teeth of the darkening, dying year. Our hearts leapt at the cry and we howled like thirsty Indians—anticipating blood and massacres.

We were still kids, to the marrow, so we worshipped snow, and driving and shopping and getting to work and other excuses for resenting the white of reality were far from our hearts.

"I can smell it in the air. I can smell it already!" one of the guys yelled.

Big guys, little guys, in-between guys—we were *the guys* of 81st Street, the most glorious block, the most glorious spot on earth.

Eighty-first Street! What a ring it has to it! Why, it sends a "t'rill" through my heart even now. With its rows of nearly identical flat-faced brick houses, its stoops, its gardens, its immense ailanthus trees.

Oh 81st, you were a charmed street, prestigious, a one-and-only, the envy of all other streets. Before your houses proper began, up the block by Sirico's Pizzeria and Summer Garden, you gave us the perfect punchball and stickball field.

The trees started much further down, so there was lots of room for towering fly balls. Sewer covers—in the center of the street—provided an official measure for balls hit or races run. The slope of 81st was perfect, too, somewhere between flat and a hill, great for running games and roller-skating and hockey. We were the chosen of the neigh-borhood and any time we booked up a big game with teams from other blocks we always wound up playing on 81st Street.

We rarely lost.

When Christmas

came to 81st Street

our houses

decked themselves

in lights.

There were

the blue-light people,

the white-light people

and

the twinkly-light people—

inviting our dim, run-down world to step

into the refreshment of the light—a world just

around the corner.

Mr. Caruso had Santa and sleigh and a herd of reindeer galloping across his yard. Somebody said he liked sleighing reindeer because he was a butcher. I don't know about that, but he did like meat and he ate enough of it while other families were scarfing down pastafazool to clog his pipes so tight with fat he died before he was 50.

The only bleak, blank house on the block belonged to Mrs. Scarpaci, who had a quarrel with the light. She resented Christmas and all boys and girls and living beings. With her twisted bun and flaring nostrils and stark black stockings, she wove a darksome cloud around her house. She kept only one bare bulb on at a time. But not even Mrs. Scarpaci could dim the triumph of those confetti-colored lights.

People used to come on pilgrimage to see the lights of 81st, cruising past in their cars, or on foot, pointing and oogling. We were the luckiest kids in Brooklyn—and in the whole world, too, if you really want to know.

Nobody told me this but I hugged a secret surmise that our glimmerous display was there, mostly, to guide St. Nicholas, his sled and flying reindeer, to a pin-point landing on 81st Street.

As the magical time drew near, I noticed a mysterious air, like a fat, furry, hazy-blue cat, curling about our house. Stealthy, surreptitious deeds transpired behind closed doors. Bulky bags were being brought in from the cold. And I was being warned to stay out of closets. Our house had cavernous closets, too, filled to overflowing with coats and hats and clothes and shoes and boxes and bags and all manner of skeletons from many a Christmas past.

But I wasn't interested in closets and whatever presents were hidden in them. After all, somebody bought those presents, so they didn't mean very much. I could wait till Christmas morning for those.

The presents I cared about were the ones that came from a workshop at the North Pole. Those were the real presents. Those were the things I really wanted, or even better, things I didn't realize I wanted that Santa, in his benevolent wisdom, thought I should have.

In those final calendar-crossing days before Christmas I labored over my letter to Santa Claus, giving him the gist of my wishes by listing a load of possibilities. Whoever passed by and saw me sweating so mightily at writing and re-writing invariably noted how different my attitude was from the one I exhibited when confronting my homework. When they really wanted to rile me they would wave a finger at me and hum fragments of a song about being naughty or nice.

Santa Claus' coming to town was no laughing matter. We were all on our best behavior in December. Bless his cheeks, Santa never left coal in my stocking, not even in my most dastardly years. He was more about mercy than justice.

My kid sister usually needed my help when

she wrote her letter to Santa, and I usually made her ask Santa for something for me. I knew that wasn't quite kosher but she didn't mind because her letters were too short, anyway.

Anxiety was hammering out a towering town in our house. My mother, whose real name was Benedetta (Betty for short) was getting more anxious, and getting migraines more often. She bickered with my father more often, too. His name was Nicholas, Nicola Santa to be exact (Nick or Nicky, for short) and nothing ruffled him—supposedly.

The skirmishing between them revolved around the Christmas tree my father had not yet bought. Matters got so black, threats of buying an artificial tree were thrown around like flaming spears.

Dad was stalling for the right time, and Christmas Eve was that time. We were bound to buy the tree and decorate it on the very same night. That was the tradition passed down from his father and that's what he was determined to do. This made the familial road unnecessarily bumpy, although that never deterred my father from forging ahead towards something—anything—he had set his mind on.

A

esthetics

was my mother's

great concern—for her

the worst aspersion cast

upon a tree—ours or anyone else's— was that

it

was

skimpy.

"Skimpy." *That* was the word! Skimpiness was the pit of all possible faults. We dreaded a skimpy tree, too, not merely on the grounds of it being an aesthetic outrage but because it meant my dear mother was discontented, and when my mother was discontented she fell into a mood, and when my mother was in a mood it was murder. And the last thing we wanted was murder on Christmas Eve.

So on behalf of peace-on-earth and reverence for human life, and in the hope of rescuing this Christmas from the clutches of calamity, I kept nudging my father:

"When are we gonna get the tree, Dad?"

"Go do something."

"I *am* doing something; I'm talking to you." My tongue flicked quick in those days.

"You're bothering me, Mr. Smarts," he said. "Bothering is not talking."

My father was busy in his printing shop in the cellar, setting type for some fancy wedding invitations. His green eye-shade gave his bony face an unearthly tint.

"Everybody else has their tree, Dad," I moaned.

"I don't care about *everybody else*." Peering through his eye-shade at me, he said, "And you shouldn't either."

"Mommy says we're gonna have *no* Christmas tree this year before she gets a skimpy one!"

Slowly, he shook his head like one grown hopelessly weary of the invincible stupidity of humankind. He sucked some air through his incisors and whispered the clincher, "Don't we always end up with a beautiful tree?"

We did, I had to admit it, but that was only because my mother was inspired—a midnight genius—and she could make even an old clothes-tree shine. Plus, we had balls, crates of them, and bubble lights and well-lit cottages and gaudy porcelain figurines and big wigs of angel hair and tinsel galore.

But we always risked a skimpy, disaster-stricken tree. Had we gone out like everybody else did, when they were plentiful, we would have had our pick—like everybody else. Then, of course, we wouldn't have had the thrill of such high drama.

So we fiddled and faddled until the wooden sidewalk racks outside Bova's Grocery and Aiello's Pork Store on 80th Street and Maggie's Pastry Shop on 79th, and all the gypsy places down 13th Avenue were picked clean, including the immense parking lot by the Knights of Columbus, and then and only then would the family sally forth, my father's jaw set, determined to get his "bargain." And, my father could bargain like a horse trader, and so he did.

My sister and brother and I blushed to the gills with all the haggling we heard and by the crusty edge that got into my father's voice. We tried to wander off, feigning interest in wreaths or tree-stands, but my mother yanked us back. Ultimately, though, in the cold, in the bone-biting and finger-chewing cold—for Christmas Eve invariably took a turn for the bitter—through the tar-black, panther-black, bible-black night, we hauled our tree home.

It was a miserable tree, one nobody else wanted—lop-sided, too small, top broken off, gap-toothed spaces between branches—with a re-grettable, inevitable broad swath of skimpiness.

My father reassured us all the way home.

"We turn the bad side to the corner. Who's gonna see back there? Who's even gonna look? Betty, listen to me ... Betty ..."

"This is the last year I get a skimpy tree," she croaked portentously. "I'm warning you. I'm warning you *all*."

I didn't like the sound of my mother's warnings.

It was a glum trudge home, crowded with schemes of how I might find another family to live with. Episodes like this confirmed what I had heard snickered and sworn to a hundred times over.

> *Yes, yes, of course it is true, it has to be true:*
> *there had been a mix-up at the hospital—*
> *a tragic mix-up!*
> *Somewhere—out there—*
> *in the sprawl and spread*
> *of the borough of Brooklyn*
> *were my authentic parents.*
> *Out in Flatbush, maybe, or even Canarsie!*
> *No, no, how could I be the result of these two?*
> *I don't even look like them!*
> *Just like they said—my parents are Chinese.*
> *My eyes have a slant to prove it.*

My mother's mood hung heavy upon us till we got home, where my grandmother, waiting at the door, a bowl in one hand, rolling pin in the other, swept her up into the last-minute dinner preparations.

So, while my father—and I, his resistant assistant—climbed upstairs to prop up our skimpy tree in its wobbly stand . . .

. . . my grandmother began
whipping Christmas Eve
to its culmination,

and its culmination was . . .

a sublime extravaganza!

Grandma's cooking could bring wolves out of the woods, make barbarians civil, and turn the heads of proud, adventurous men away from all high endeavor. Around Christmastime, we always had soup lines of freeloaders at our door, lured mostly I suspect by Grandma's culinary sleight-of-hand. I was easy prey myself. Once her multifarious fragrances bushwhacked me upstairs, they'd pick me up, and send me bounding downstairs like Bojangles—two at a time.

She was in her faded blue apron with the pink peonies on it and she was striding about like a field marshal. She had my grandfather hand-rolling batches of "stroofula," little doughballs deep-fried and dipped in honey and glorified with colorful sprinkles. And she had my mother and Aunt Grace working at the main sweet of the season, a pastry that went by the ominous-sounding name of *een-gart-a-debt*.

The creation and production of ingartadette was a daring affair. The dough was rolled out on wide gray slabs of marble by mighty rolling pins with painted red handles—yellow warmish dough that tasted good just as it was. The dough was then cut into parallelograms, and one by one, given a twist and skittled into hot oil. Adroitly, when they'd reached a golden brown, my mother would pluck them out with a long-pronged fork. When they were cool, some were jumbled in powdered sugar and some drowned in a dark, delectable juice decocted from honey and prunes and raisins. The ones soaked in

juice turned purple and delicate as iris petals, becoming more succulent as the days promenaded toward the New Year.

She was relentless, my grandmother. She held the whole holiday and the whole family together. When she died at 92 the glue came undone and the family fell to pieces. While she was alive she carried us through good times and bad. But it was in the bad times—like the Depression—that she really showed her stuff.

She was the one who took the subway to The City to get the goods for the family to do "homework." In those days many an Italian fresh off the boat, not yet Americanized and afraid of work, brought work home from the local factories, and whole families labored together into the wee hours.

Grandma brought back the orders and raw material for fancy white embroidered collars to be sewn onto dresses, and "frogs"—button loops made out of piping—for ladies' coats, and great spools of hemming and beading and sequinning.

The bead-and-sequin work, Grandma's specialty, took the longest and the most care. But it netted the most money. Intently, step by step, she showed us how to do it all, and kept checking us to be sure it was perfect. Her work was never rejected by the companies, like some of my great-aunts' and cousins'. And when we met our quota, she'd lug it back to The City in two stout shopping bags.

Without her at the helm, the family would never have weathered the Depression and the War as well as it did. My grandfather, a farmer in the old country, peddled ice, and later, coal, but he never turned a decent buck. She pulled us through, her and her homework.

When I got old enough to help, the family was busy homeworking pocketbooks—milk-white women's pocketbooks made of shiny plastic squares sewn firmly together. From a distance, the homework business might seem picturesque, but back then I was mortally ashamed of it, so much so that when my friends came up to the house I'd hide the paraphernalia under the couch; and when

I was wrestling with polio and condemned to spend eternities in bed, I'd shove the works under the blankets. I figured my friends had enough ways to razz me without tacking ladies' handbags to the list.

We made piles of them and piles on them—those chintzy bags. Funny, though, how the irony of making pocketbooks in hard times never struck us. Grandma kept us all at it. Even me. Even my Aunt Grace who always had better things to do, like looking for a husband.

At 9 o'clock, on the hallowed eve of Christmas, my grandfather emerged with a tray heaped high with the clams he'd pried open, a sign that the night's festivities were officially underway.

Yessir, I remember them all, every last uncle and aunt and cousin, and the excitement of their arrival, and how my aunts' perfume reached us upstairs before anything else. Uncle Vito—known throughout the western world as "Bates"—handsome, dashing, mustachioed, the life of the party, with his gloomy wife Rose; Uncle Mike—the flat-footed busdriver who invariably fell asleep with the Sunday funnies on his face, forever insisting he was just resting his eyes; his wife Anne—short but high-bosomed, who settled for Mike because she couldn't get Bates; my godfather—Uncle Nickie, suave as George Raft, with his wife Caroline—statuesque but with too many teeth in her mouth and Aunt Grace—with whatever sailor she'd managed to scrape off the streets—and all the kids who had come head-over-heels out of the cornucopia of the years—

Frankie
& Diana
& Andrew
& Annie
& Frankie
& Diane
& Don
& Frankie . . .

Not to forget my sister Rina, and my button-nosed brother Dennis. Rina was four years younger than me then, and Dennis, ten. They still are, of course. Rina, named after my grandmother Caterina, always beautiful, has grown more so with each full loop of the planet. And Dennis has become a lot more handsome, distinguished, upstanding—and a lot more bald. We were all there, at one time or another. One big family. One big table. One big feast.

After the raw clams came steaming platters of macaroni and broccoli—lavished with garlic and olive oil and salty little anchovies—followed by fried shrimp, fried flounder filet, and then my grandmother's incomparable, legendary—onion pie!

Then before our dazzled eyes, in mouth-watering procession, marched baked clams and eel, fried or broiled, and soaked with lemon-and-oil, and calamar, which we used to call devil-fish, and vinegared scungill, or sea-snail, and salad and celery and fennel and fruit—apples, oranges, pomegranates—and hot chestnuts and walnuts (always walnuts) and pizza dolce, panettone and struffoli and, finally, ingartadette.

When we were done, and we knew what it was to be stuffed, and aunts and uncles had scattered to their respective houses, there was still the tree to trim.

With Rina and Dennis tucked in for the night, Mom and Dad and I worked on into the wee hours, painstakingly stirring our tired spruce into splendor. Oh, there were gleaming spheres in that tree—flying angels—alluring shadow worlds, wherein swords of light clashed with darkness.

As midnight approached, I found myself drowning in dreams, wishful dreams of leaping up early enough one of those Christmases and catching you-know-who in the act, seeing him with my own eyes—meeting him head-on.

He was the one I longed to know. He was the force of good and giving personified. He was my childhood's great reality.

I believed in him.

But there'd been a rumor. We had more than one vicious argument on the streets over it, too.

"There ain't no Santa Claus . . ."

How my insides trembled at the sacrilege, the unforgivable blasphemy of it all.

"They just made him up! He ain't real!"
"Ha ha, Frankie still believes in Santa!"
"He ain't ree-yul, Frankie!
He ain't ree-yule!"

The thought went like a Roman broadsword through my tender heart. Stricken, I tore the words out of my mind, words—like a manslaughtering, cold-tongued sea.

I don't want to think about whether he exists or not.
I want to think about what he is doing.
That's right, what he does.
What he brings, his work.
That's what matters.
Santa can't be erased so easily.
He was—he is—alive in the heart of the world.

42

And I'll find him. I'll surprise him one night.
What will I say? What will he say?
Will he be stern—cross with me?
Suppose I'm never supposed to meet him . . .
But I want to see him—face to face.
Why? So I can know who he is.
Why? So I can help him with his work.
Why? Because I want to, because I want to.
But why?
Because, because,
just because . . .

Back then, decorating that skimpy old tree, I realized I neither knew nor could do hardly anything. Everything was a mystery—like the one about where I had come from. Granted, I didn't know for sure what St. Nicholas' work was, but I knew it was more than handing out presents and checking if we were naughty or nice. It was some great work, wide as the world.

Oh, I pictured myself out there with him, riding on the Great Sled, deer hooves scattering snowdust, the wind stinging my cheeks to a rosiness, just like his.

Now I know this—my youthful yearnings were bringing me to the threshold of the vast cavern of the heart where all the meaning of life is stored—where all the children are and all the lost luster and longing is—where truth is, and hope is, and delight sings upon every tree branch.

And out of the heart's core, he comes!
He comes, with a twinkle,
to restore us to the golden land of lost delight,
reminding everyone,
girls and boys,
grownups and elders.
Though nights come,
bleak, black and wintry,
and terrible deeds are wrought,
and strife, meanness and greed seem to hold sway—
he watches always, the one, the only one,

turning dark into light,
suffering into meaning,
sorrow into joy,
and all things into glory.

Despite my valiant efforts at decorating Ol' Skimpy, my eyelids drooped, and the tide of dreams dragged me off. My mother noticed, and she banished me to bed.

The night before Christmas was the time I was told-retold-cajoled-commanded—more fiercely than any other night—to "Get to bed!" Going to bed early meant you got up early and opened presents and played. But more importantly, it was the way to safeguard your relationship to Santa Claus, who, if he happened to come down your chimney a bit ahead of schedule and didn't find you in bed, snuggled in sugar-plum dreams, would pass your house by.

Alas, I never went early to bed. Even when I was older and I knew I was going to be roused at the crack of dawn by my two ever-eager, wide-eyed sons, I never dropped onto my pillow till my back ached and my eyes bulged and burned like two sore bellybuttons.

Much to my despair, this Christmas night had me wound so with desperate expectations I tossed and twisted, entangling myself in the covers until I was as immobilized as Gulliver on the strand of Lilliputia. But I couldn't make myself sleep.

I had been forewarned I would be extremely "over-tired," and sure enough—my parents were right again. Yet, being privy to the folklore of childhood I knew—as a last resort—even the highest hero, having exhausted his inexhaustible resources, will stoop to counting sheep. So I, too, began to count.

Every so often, my mother appeared at the door, hissing menacingly. "You're still not asleep?! You'd better get to sleep!"

"I'm trying," I assured her with my best sleepy-mouth. She had no idea how hard I was trying.

At some dimensionless point—when my flock of muttonheads got woozy and dallied and gaped perversely at the hurdles they were required to leap, they swelled and lifted off the ground, against all laws rational and scientific, and hung in the air, fat and fluffy, like dirigibles, some even sprouting wings and soaring off to inacces-sible places—I took the bait and went to wherever good sleepers go.

And in that state all was well.

There's a time in the very belly of Christmas Eve
when every breathing thing drops to its knees
and the starry wheels stop short . . .
and all the universe stands still,
and the silence that congregates then
is raucous enough
to wake the dead—
and that night
the silence
awakened
me.

I had to pee, too, and as fate would have it, I couldn't hold it in. I rolled over, kicking and writhing my way out of the grip of my covers.

I could hardly see. My eyes were hazed by the residue of vague dreams. I shuffled heedlessly to the toilet trying to blink them clear. I kept them half-closed, half-hoping—hypocritically—I wouldn't run into St. Nick.

For a flash I thought the living room light was on. No—it was the tree lights. Still on. And they were never left on—certainly not overnight, not even on Christmas Eve. Santa had his own flashlight— I'd been told—and he didn't need us to waste good electricity.

And though I tried my best not to see them, and after I'd seen them I pretended I hadn't, I saw PRESENTS under the tree!

But that wasn't all—I saw somebody! A person! Leaving the living room! Even if I hadn't seen him I would have known it—because I could feel it, I could feel the PRESENCE— of whoever had been there. And I knew who it was who had been there!

I knew.

With my two-fisted heart pummeling the inside of my chest and my breath coming in gulps, I scanned the room. *He's in the house.*
Chilly waters were trickling down to my toes.
He's in my house!
Santa Claus himself is,
    yes, in my own house!
     I surprised him!
My own breath corked my throat.
      We nearly met—and spoke. I had nearly
       had what no other boy or girl had ever had
     in the entire history of the world. What I had
     been hoping for had nearly happened.
      No, it had happened—almost! Yes! Yes!
    but he's still here! So, scared as I was,
I dashed across the living room,
   my thoughts dashing along behind me.
   What would he be like—
    what would he say—
     would he scold me—
      punish me—
       would he wipe me off his list?

When I reached the foyer I thought I had lost him.
 But no. *There—he must have stepped into the closet—that's*
 what had happened—that's where he'd gone—the closet with
 the metal ladder in it—the ladder that went to the roof.
 Oh, he was quick—slippery as silk.
 How could I have missed him?!
  He was here; I was here.
   The door—the dark door, chestnut-brown and
     shellacked, was closed tight.
      He should have waited for me.
      Why couldn't he wait?
      I could have touched him.
      I could have talked to him . . .
   I listened for a moment
    for the sound of footsteps,
    or hoofbeats on the roof,
    but there was only the night,
    holding its breath.
   But maybe, my mind mumbled,
 he's still in the closet.
 I put my hand on the knob . . .

My parents' bedroom, situated across the hall from the closet, had its door wide open. I didn't want to wake them. No, not till morning. I thought to close it. I wavered between the doors. Short—sweet—that was the way. I resolved—with the three o'clock courage boys of Brooklyn sometimes summon—I resolved to yank open the closet door—and know—once and for all. Which is what I did.

What I found was a darkness so packed with coats that a snake couldn't get through, let alone a fat man. Baffled by his stealth, I lingered, the brass doorknob in my hand cold as a frog's belly. I put my forehead to the door and leaned on it until it clicked shut.

When I glanced into the dark of my parents' room, another thought took shape—he might have skipped in there. He might be in there now, standing in the dark.

But nature was calling hysterically. The bowl-top was down—as it shouldn't have been—and the floor got wet—more than could dry by the morning. By the time I was done swabbing up the mess I'd made, a hundred Santa Clauses could have paraded in and out of the house.

I snapped on my parents' light anyway—there they were, none but them, my mother and father, face up with that angelic look closed eyes give to even the most callous criminals. I turned off the light and stood there a while, glad they were my parents.

I went slouching back to bed. Yet down the arches of that long night, I found myself fleeing from the hounding suspicion that it was my father who had been in the living room, my own father, and that there had never been a Santa Claus at all. Ever.

But the magic of that Christmas morn brushed aside my cloud of doubts. Under the tree was everything I had asked for and more, just as there had always been throughout the years. Well, not everything I asked for—everything I wanted. I always asked for a sack-full of presents, trusting Santa could tell which ones I really wanted.

Christmas morning,
oh Christmas morning!

Your freshness shames the springtime.

Your crisp innocence,

Your sweet hopefulness,

Your fullness, like a dear promise kept.

Oh, if I could have all my Christmas mornings

Rolled up again, into a ball,

You could keep the years, all of them.

And if my life was made of Christmas mornings

I'd have the life I've always wanted.

To awaken as the world snores.

To hear the house poised and expectant, cracking its

floorboards like they were knuckles.

I sit up. I am one harmonious sense—

eyes wide, ears perked—

AWAKE.

My heart swells inside me.

And outside a great hush holds all of Brooklyn

in its fond embrace.

I peer through the blinds
and there is the snow,
soft and tender,
compassionately absorbing
the least crackle.
Draped carefully—
on every nub and picket
of the fences, over the fat thighs
of the sycamore outside my window,
on the stoops and gardens,
on sidewalks and streets,
over the cars,
over my grandfather's mulberry tree—
like a mischievous giant
whom nothing and no one can gainsay,
sprawling grandiosely
across property—public and private—
king of the winter.

The fat sun came up smiling that Christmas day, flinging sparkles off the crystalline robe of snow. I have hopes it is the right kind of snowfall. I hope, I hope. I toss away the covers. I swing my feet onto the frigid floorboards—the scatter rug is rarely in the right spot. The heat isn't up yet. Before I get my slippers on, the radiators start to clear their throats. I can smell the comfort of the coming heat. Throwing open the window I scoop up snow from the sill, taste some, test some and squeeze some into a ball.

"Good packing, oh boy, oh boy, good packing," I gloat, fiendishly.

I rear back and hurl one—side-arm—at George Durand's fancy green Buick. With a resounding *pffud* it sticks to his back fender, leaving a round white bull's eye. George, who lives to gnash his teeth, is going to be livid! Ah, there was such good packing in those days!

Now I'm in the living room—as exuberant as a kid tumbleweeding down a hill. The lights on the tree are off. Who turned them off? I plug in the lights, and abandoning all thoughts about who and where and why and when, I yip like a cowboy and dive into the silvery joy of Christmas. Presents keep me present.

All at once in a vision I see—

careening down the coal-chute of the cheery years—all my Christmas gifts: the toy soldiers, the cowboy outfit, the six-gun with a revolving barrel, the car you pump with your feet, the scooter, the tricycles, the bicycles, the books—*Tom Sawyer* and *Penrod* and *Robinson Crusoe* and *Twenty Thousand Leagues Under the Sea,* and roller skates and ice skates and the basketball and the Philco radio of honey-colored wood and the grey Pentron tape recorder that made a wah-wah sound and had to be sent back to the shop again and again and still never worked right—so that I cursed all machines and the dullness of men's ears that couldn't hear the wah-wah or the hardness of their hearts that insisted on denying it—and the airplane, a bright canary-yellow Piper Cub, steered in flight with strings like a marionette but which I couldn't put together, but which my Uncle Nickie and my father spent every evening through New Year's constructing, and of course, there were the boats—an endless flotilla of ships, square-riggers and junks, clippers and galleons, motor boats and tugs and submarines, too, and ocean liners and aircraft carriers and battleships . . .

But all my great gains are mingled in my mind now. I can't truly tell if the gifts I got were the gifts I got or the gifts I wished for and never got, or if they were gifts I gave my own children. The lines between what was, what might have been, what I yearned for or experienced in dreams, are gossamer.

Sometimes, when I'm weary of well-doing, I wonder what's the good of getting things if you can't remember what you got? Or what's worse: thinking you got things you never got at all? Where is the source of the rivers of desire, and into what far-off oceans do they run?

In one way or another I got what I wanted, as do we all, but not without paying a very dear price. For, like a cruel shadow, running alongside the sweet anticipation of Christmas Day, was the agonizing uncertainty of: Will I *get* what I asked for? Will I *get* what I want?

Alas, in those days, I thought my happiness depended on getting what I wanted; now I see that happiness depends on wanting what I get.

That Christmas I found myself surrounded by a bounty of boxes, ready to revel in the novelty of them all. But I wanted my parents there, too.

I had given them each something: a tieclasp for my father, that I bought, as we used to say, "with my own money" (which rings rather ludicrous considering how hard it is to hold on to anything in a world of such white-watery flux, on top of which dollars-and-I have had such an on-again, off-again relationship these many a year) and for my mother I got a pair of pearl-colored knitting needles in a round Quaker Oats box on which I had pasted a print of some powder-puffed figures, on swings and things, who were behaving fuzzily and so ridiculously French. My mother liked such people, particularly when they held up lamps and jewelry boxes.

"Mom, wake up! Dad, wake up! Wake up!" I had to rouse them, whether they wanted to or not—"Merry Christmas! You have to come see what Santa Claus left me!"

I said something like that every year when I shook them awake. This time, this most particular Christmas morning, my words sounded a little hollow. But I coaxed and shook them anyway. We had presents to open, regardless.

"You got presents, too!"

Opening presents in pajamas, that is, while *you* are in pajamas, has to be one of the most quaint and quintessential, old-fashioned American pleasures—like riding a Schwinn bicycle or watching the pretty girl waiting and weeping at the garden gate for the handsome boy who, alas, will not be returning from our latest overseas war.

Not all my presents were splendid, though.

I got neckties, one, two, or three each year—fat and creatively ugly—of red and green and purple murk, with unspeakable paleolithic parameciums skidding across them, ties to make a small boy wail to heaven for mercy. But it was the Forties, and some people thought it was good taste, I suppose.

There was one other present.

I got one of these each year, each year without fail, from the time my pants began to sport pockets. These were unquestionably not from Santa himself, for they were wrapped and had tags on them with a *To: Frankie, Love: Mom and Dad* in my mother's graceful handwriting. Always a quaint white box, always some onion-skin paper, and always the same intoxicating aroma, with a staid confirmation in embossed gold letters guaranteeing GENUINE LEATHER.

I wondered why I needed a wallet. I suppose my poor parents were trying to give me a message. But how many wallets can one boy use? Rightly or wrongly, I attribute my abiding disinterest in all things green to those early wallet-littered years. I sold them all, all my aromatic wallets, or I bartered them on the open market for worthwhile things, like marbles or guns or baseball cards.

Though I tried to hold back time, the church bells clanged and I had to rush and dress, for the whole family went to church on Christmas Day—even my father, who despised what he called the "black robes," and my grandfather, too, serious as a bullfrog in his double-breasted suit and mousey fedora, and my grandmother, bustling exactly as she did when she went shopping at the A&P—except on the holidays she veiled her comely, defiant face with a swatch of black fishnet.

Marching woodenly up the block in our church costumes we met The Faithful coming out of their holes, and up on the avenue, streams of them brawling, colliding, eddying, in choppy flow to and from *la nostra chiesa*, our church. It was just like Easter—in full regalia they came, dressed to the hilt, dressed to the teeth, and in some cases, quite obviously, dressed to kill.

I remember thinking how fine a thing church must be for masses of men to leave the place with looks of such blessed relief on their faces.

We suffering children were elbowed into the gutter so the stampeding grown-up Christians might pass.

Nay, they were more than Christians—they were "Cath-o-licks." Thirteenth Avenue was a snarl of them—on the sidewalks, on the street. That so many emerged on Christmas Sunday was a tribute to the Faith, and a testimony to the unwavering devotion of dear Dyker Heights, a paragon among Italo-American neighborhoods.

The Shrine Church of St. Bernadette was famous among bishoprics and mafiosi, and from its nave flowed a wondrous river of charity, its tinkling waters rising to floodtide at the feasts of the Nativity and the Resurrection.

Hard as we tried, our parish never scored first in the diocese. Whenever *The Tablet*, our Catholic tabloid, trumpeted the totals, we always came up an infuriating second. Yet, considering how hard-working and tight-fisted the Italian immigrants and their descendants were, it was an annual miracle of the first water.

The monetary miracle of St. Bernadette's was performed indefatigably by the infamous and well-loathed Monsignor Francis X. Barella. As his name proclaims, he was the barrel-bellied, bull-roaring builder of St. Bernadette's who alternately harangued and terrorized his parishioners to uncharted heights of generosity.

Our church was a simple, neo-Gothic structure, featuring a grotto over the high altar, with the figure of a kneeling Bernadette gazing up at a poised and smiling lady in white and blue, above whose loveliness appeared the enigmatic words:

I Am The Immaculate Conception

The huge wooden folding doors dividing the church from the hall—home to basketball and bingo, and all manner of meetings—were pushed back at the big Sunday masses and the great church feasts. On the Lord's Birthday, they revealed a jammed and heaving house.

Those who'd come early and "grabbed" seats lived to rcgrct it, for the dear ushers fulfilled their duty to the God-of-All-Things-Including-Sardines by packing people in pews till they oozed oil. Once every body, fat and skinny, had re-arranged their rumps after the last onslaught, down the aisle came strutting our two ushers—pompous and officious—with yet another sardine or two. Only when their torturous packing was scrupulously complete were latecomers, mercifully, allowed to loiter in the rear.

For us, the kids of the land, the whole affair was agonizing. We had dragged ourselves there, under duress, at great cost-of-time-and-better-things-to-do, for some heavenly purpose, or so we assumed, but instead found ourselves squashed and poked, with our view blocked by ponderous ladies in ten-gallon hats. In those ancient times, ladies and their like were obliged to wear hats in church (while men were required to expose the sheen of bald, balder and baldest pates). Many a lady wore fur, too, with fox-faces hanging limply on their shoulders, and most had waded to the knees in Parisian toilet water. Yea, Codfish Mighty! The reek in those pews made it a trial worthy of the early desert fathers.

We fidgeted behind the heads in hats, the scalps, the pimpled necks, occasionally catching a glimpse of the backs of glistening priests in red and gold vestments. There was much long-winded chanting and a surplus of bell-jingling before the reading of the gospel, our first chance to stretch. Eventually came the dread moment when Monsignor Barella rolled over to the microphone.

"My dear friends . . ."

That's how he always started. But we weren't his dear friends. He had dear friends within the police force and dear friends among the mob, but I doubt he ever had a dear friend in the pews. He was renowned in the Heights for his nepotism and nefarious real estate transactions.

"My dear mothers and fathers and blessed children and grandfathers and grandmothers," he went on in a wet and casky voice.

"Now we have arrived at that season, that season of giving, the blessed Christmas season when the baby Jesus comes to birth in our hearts and the spirit of St. Nicholas rules the day."

"Yes, my friends, we have come to that special time—and we all knew what special time he meant—that *most special* time, my dear friends, when we can, and must, and wish to show the Almighty and Merciful God, from the generous depths of our hearts, in a very special way, how very much we love these orphans of Brooklyn, His beloved orphans, His little ones, who are so very, very special to Him."

Grating as his homiletic style was it was hard to ignore the orphans of Brooklyn, linked as they were to God and Christ and the spirit of St. Nick. My heart even softened to the good monsignor as he went on specializing, driving us all drowsy until, with a great snort, he pounded upon the pulpit and bellowed—

"I want a silent collection! Do you hear me, my dear friends? Mothers and grandmothers—fathers and grandfathers—godmothers and godfathers."

Angrily, he pounded again! I glanced down the rows of parishioners. They looked as blank and motionless as racks of clothing.

"I said a silent collection!!" and his fists beat out a suitable climax.

Then with an abrupt shift to oil and obsequiousness, he concluded:

"How Almighty God will bless each and every one of you for all, I say all, of your remaining days. And so, my dear friends, when our blessed ushers—come down, gentlemen, and begin at the front—when our ushers place their collection baskets before your generous breasts, let your pocketbooks and your wallets open as wide as your blessed hearts."

Beaming toothily, arms outspread, the monsignor blessed us in his very special way.

"No silver, no copper, not a tinkle my friends. Let us have nothing but a holy and special silence."

Though he never actually said damn your hides, when he was done it sure felt like it. The hush of a funeral parlor descended upon the crowd. The ushers stalked and stretched their baskets solemnly. We all strained to hear if any dared violate the silent music of the collection.

The creeping collection and the plodding pace of the rest of the mass ended at last in a flurry of bells, and we scrambled out onto the streets and I got back to the open-ended rumpus of Christmas.

Later, when the church was empty
and the hurly-burly of the Masses done
and the deep peace in the marble and mortar
of the place had once more folded its wings,
we went back to visit the manger.
We were supposed to pray,
but mostly I just knelt there,
inhaling the fragrance of the straw,
and admiring the Wise Men
and their curly beards,
and the livestock,
and the clean-cut,
blue-eyed babe
who remained ever
with arms wide,
reaching heartwise
and trustingly
towards us.
I closed my eyes
and listened to the stillness
and the click of old ladies' heels
echoing in the sanctuary.

Back home, later still, when my father was busy and my mother distracted, I slipped into my snowsuit and galoshes and searched out my friends. One at a time they toppled out of their houses, and we gamboled in the snow till we were dank and bone-weary.

As the afternoon slumped down to a fiery sunset we dug ourselves an igloo in the belly of one of the great white mountains and we poked up a chimney hole and we sat around a fire till the roof melted away, dumping down on us like a truckload of dreams. Above us was a navy-blue sky alive and prinking with stars that looked amazingly like the sequins on my mother's favorite Christmas-blue dress. By the shafts of starlight, too soon for streetlights, we draggled home with wet necks and soggy hearts to our varied but matching destinies.

The family had come back to life and was eating again. Another enormous meal, with leftovers in profusion, and cakes and fruit and the piercing bouquet of my mother's perculator coffee. My father and Uncle Nickie were arguing about their favorite subject—President Roosevelt and the mendacities of politics.

Aunt Grace was dancing with her sailor. Grandma was rushing back and forth issuing commands. Grandpa was bringing out his favorite game. Magnanimously, he summoned us all to the table, and handed out his numbered Lotto cards.

He had a cigar box with a hole in it. With a noisy, exhilarating shake, out came bobbling the button-sized pieces of real wood with raised, red-painted numbers on them. He loved calling out the numbers.

"Fifty-seven-a . . ."

"Thirty-two-a . . ."

"Six-a-teen-a . . ."

"Nine-a . . ."

"Twenty-five-a . . ."

After a while, and one too many losses, I sneaked upstairs, evading my mother's eagle eye, relieved to be free of the pressures of winning and losing on Christmas night, and once more at rest in the mellow peace of our parlor, back in my pajamas again, I gazed up at our beautiful, skimpy tree for a long time.

Ah, when I was a boy in Brooklyn
        and my heart was full of Christmas,
            there was no home for me but where I was—
                there, upon that soft maroon rug
            embellished with lilies and roses,
                golden fringes all around and the great red sofa,
                    and two bosomy, overstuffed armchairs,
                        royal blue and damask,
        and the fallacious fireplace, trimmed with fool's gold,
            and the real logs burning in a fake fire,
                and the great oval mirror on a silken rope
                    and the petite, glass-topped coffee table
                        with the milk-glass candy dish trimmed
                            in old rococco gold,
        and the stately, grand-globed floor lamp
            that shone brighter with each turn of the switch,
            and the green, gleaming Tree of Life
                my Mom and Dad had turned into
                    an ever-sparkling tree,
                        flashing with the unimaginable insights
                            of the archangels in Paradise.

That was the Christmas—oh, how well I remember it—when Santa eluded me and when, thank God and all his holy, twinkling stars, I found him again. My eyes surged with tears because I knew how lucky I was. I was swept up on a wave of ache and wonder, a kindly wave that turned loss of innocence into unexpected ripeness.

When my eyes dried I went down once more to my grandparents' basement. Excitement was at the full. The cigar box was rattling and Grandpa's voice was ringing. Aunt Grace and her sailor had just won the pot. Grandpa's face was flushed and beaming—for he liked the sailor.

I took a card or two and sat between my Mom and Dad and we played Lotto into the wee hours. Some of us lost, and some of us won, and some of us broke even. But we all got tired and, at the end, we all went to bed.

I stayed awake though, listening to the friendly sizzle of the steam, and watching the venetian-blind pattern passing car lights threw onto the ceiling.

I lay there, aglow with what the great day had brought, long after the kitchen lights went out and the old house had stopped creaking.

I slipped slowly,
into the warm arms of sleep,
grateful for the grace
that let me glimpse,
oh so gently,
    the real meaning of Christmas,
       and led me at last
          to the simple secret
            that Santa Claus,
              the real St. Nicholas,
                lived in my own house,
                  and heart.

Best Wishes

. . . and Buon Natale

My Grandmother and Grandfather

Recipes

"Here are three treasured recipes
of my grandmother,
Diana Casamassima Tarulli,
who immigrated to New York in 1898
at age 12.

I recorded her words exactly
as she explained and demonstrated,
step by step."

Rina Crocitto Betrò

Grandma's Onion Pie

This pie is a delectable treat used as a side dish, as an appetizer or at cocktail parties. It's 1 ½" high, and displays the white of the onions, red of the tomatoes, and complementary green of the olives. The addition of sliced black-pitted olives is optional.

Crust (Dough):
1 ½ cups of warm water
1 package of yeast
3 small potatoes skinned, boiled & mashed
3 cups of flour
1 egg yolk, beaten
1 Tbsp. salt

In a large bowl greased with oil, dissolve yeast package in warm water. To this, add potatoes, salt and flour and knead into a dough that cleans off the sides of the bowl and is not sticky. Cover and let rise in a warm place for about 3 ½ hours or until doubled in bulk. If dough is too oily, knead down again and let rise longer.

Filling:
2 ½ lbs. onions, sliced thin
2-3 Tbsp. oil
1 tsp. salt
black pepper
sliced anchovies
sliced green olives
sliced fresh or canned tomatoes (1 can)
sliced black olives (optional)
1 lb. chopped mozzarella cheese
grated pecorino romano cheese

Wash, drain and slice onions. In large pan cook onions with oil, salt, anchovies, green olives and pepper; optional: black olives. Before fully cooked, add fresh or canned tomatoes and let cook 5-10 minutes longer.

Assembly:
Divide dough into two slightly unequal parts (larger portion for bottom crust). Roll out and spread the larger portion in an oiled pie dish (13" round or 13" x 9" rectangle).

Add cooked filling, topping it with chopped mozzarella and pecorino romano grated cheese. Cover with the second crust, sealing sides firmly. Make a few 3" slits in center of top crust and brush on beaten egg yolk. Bake in 350° oven for 45 minutes, until brown.

Grandma's Ingartadette

A Christmas cookie, cut into odd shapes and fried, which just makes your mouth water as it browns in oil, then drizzled with a honey mixture and colored with sprinkles. Tasting one is like eating one potato chip—you can't refrain from eating the next.

Dough:
(Hint: Make ½ recipe)
2 lbs. flour (4 cups or more)
1 tsp. salt
1 tsp. vanilla
½ cup of vegetable shortening
1 Tbsp. brandy rum or anisette
3 eggs
1 tsp. baking powder
¾ cup of warm water
2 packages of yeast

In a bowl first mix yeast and water. Then add vegetable shortening, eggs, vanilla, and brandy. In a separate bowl mix flour, baking powder and salt. Combine the two mixtures creating a dough and knead well.

Form into balls (size of baseballs), place in a dark corner and cover with plastic wrap and towels. Let rise for 15-20 minutes. Knead one ball at a time and roll out, like a pizza, very thin.

Cut into long rectangles, round thin strips, or rosettes with pressed edges. Fry in hot deep oil, using a slotted spoon or mesh basket. As they turn golden brown, drain and remove to paper towels. Keep four batches of unfried shapes covered with cloth so they don't dry out.

Honey Mixture:
(Hint: Make ½ recipe)
1 quart of prune juice
16 ounces or more of honey
3 ½ cups of sugar

Mix all ingredients and cook until thick. Test thickness by dropping onto a dish. If a film remains on dish after removing from dish, it is thick enough. Dip fried pieces into <u>hot</u> honey mixture and drizzle over. Top with colored sprinkles.

Hint: Do not cover tray of cookies until after one day or cookies become too soft.

Filled Ungartadette:

Filling:
2 cups chopped nuts
1 cup grated chocolate or chips
3 Tbsp. anisette
1 Tbsp. cinnamon

To make filling, combine all ingredients and stir until evenly mixed.

After rolling out dough, place 1 tsp. of filling 2" apart. Fold dough over, press down edges with fork and then fry as above, and dip into honey mixture as above.

Grandma's Struffoli

Little balls piled up like a pyramid, covered with honey mixture, smelling of orange zest, sprinkled with colored sprinkles. The balls are slightly hard but sweet. The name changes according to the region of Italy in which it is made (also called Macatoli or Pinulata).

Dough:
6 eggs (beaten)
3 cups of flour
1 Tbsp. sugar
½ jigger (1 oz.) rum or anisette
vegetable oil for frying

In bowl, mix all ingredients until smooth, then knead. On a board, shape the dough into a rope ¼" thick. Slice into pieces about ¼-½" long and form into balls. Fill a heavy saucepan with oil 2-3" deep and heat the oil to 425°. Fry balls by placing them in mesh basket or colander and lowering into the hot oil. Fry until balls are lightly browned and puffed. Remove and drain on paper towels.

Topping:
16 ounces of honey
2 Tbsp. sugar
grated peel of 1 orange
multi-colored sprinkles

Combine honey and sugar in large saucepan and cook for 10 minutes. Stir in orange peel. Then add fried balls and stir quickly to coat with mixture and remove from flame.

Assembly:
Wet hands with cold water, and in pie-tin arrange balls into a pyramid shape. Top with colored sprinkles.

Buon Appetito!

A

part of
the Christmas
season I always cherish
is the *after*-Christmas, when
we savor the days of no-school,
and look forward to the next holiday,
the New Year and its Eve. The family stays
together—gifts given are tested out, worn, or
played with—wondrous feasts of leftovers come
day after day. Thankfulness for these things is the
prelude for resolution—to live life more fully, to help
others more, to make the world a better place for everyone. I am including this small piece I wrote about two
people I am especially grateful for, a little something to
share with you as you move towards
your own time of reflection,
appreciation
and intention.
Happy
New Year!

My Father and Mother

They're both gone now. While they were alive I was too busy growing up and trying to be me to honor them very much. Mostly I was trouble. I loved them, though. And like my grandmother sang to me when I was at odds with them, "Once you lose your parents you lose the best of all," I did lose the best of all. The pain of the loss of them which is supposed to diminish with the years has only gone deeper and deeper, like a splinter in the flesh of my heart.

Each New Year forces us to face what is ahead. For me the New Year will be another year without them. I remember them all the time. They seem sometimes to be hovering around me. I wish, among the many wishes bubbling up from the fountainhead of wishes in me, that this year, by my multifarious words and deeds, to bring honor to my mother and father, making up, thereby, for all the years.

My mother, she wasn't the prettiest; she wasn't the smartest; but take her for all in all, she was ever the best. In her later years her health started to go. Her heart had

95

a faulty valve which caused her to black-out a lot. She got tired easily and her voice got hoarse at the end of the day and sometimes she lost it altogether. One thing led to another.

She lived too far to visit very often. So we spoke on the phone, saying pretty much the same things: how are you feeling today, how are things going, how's the garden, how's Dad, is he behaving himself? Simple things. We liked to hear one another's voice. When I visited her she would get all excited and make an extra special tomato sauce, like rabbit sauce because she knew I liked rabbit, and special cakes like my grandmother, her mother, used to make.

But she was always thinking about me, I knew that. I felt it. It was always that way. No matter what she had on her mind, I was on her mind, too. I was her big concern. What I would study, what I would become, what I would achieve. Always something. Time and distance didn't change a thing.

So much happened, too much to go into. So much, so much since she soothed my forehead during my high and frequent fevers. So much since that first day she took my hand and brought me to school, the first of a seemingly interminable boxcar-string of days. I didn't want to go. I got sick and cried, and cried and got more sick. She didn't want me to go either. But she held my hand till the last moment and finally let it go. She bore with me through all my mistakes and mischief. She helped me with my homework into the wee hours, and God knows we had way too much of it in those days and we kids sure needed help. She wasn't always satisfied with the marks I brought home. I thought, each time that I'd done pretty well, all things considered, but she thought I was coasting. She saw a lot in me.

There were times, times through the long years, times too numerous to mention, when everything looked bleak. When action seemed futile and friends false. But, my mother was there. She was always there. Like the earth, like the sky and the sun, she was always there.

Through her came nourishment, from the milk she gave me from her own breast to the food I needed to grow and become a man, which took far too long a time. Through her came the music. Through her came the books. Through her came all the possibilities, all the faith, and all the strength.

She didn't like all my whims—wanting to be a priest and reading Thomas Merton and moving upstate and the midnight-green Cadillac I bought and the kind of teaching career I chose, that brings so little recompense, and the girls I brought home and the particular one I insisted on marrying. She, eventually, accepted them all.

Every thing I ever did mattered to her. In that great tender heart of hers she worried over me, groaned for me, prayed for me, hoped, ever hoped for me, dreading only that I might die before the promise that she saw in me came to fruit.

My mother was the perfect mother for me. We all, I suppose, get the perfect one. She knew me. She read me like a book. She said so. And she did. And yet, though I was as close to her as close can be, and have thought much about her and meditated on her, I must confess she is still to me an incomprehensible being, a mystery vast as Nature Herself. She is that original, loving, all-embracing, warm, mysterious majesty—Mother.

And I know that though I became a man and passed beyond her immediate care, and married and fathered children and tried to do a few things to justify my existence, when she left the earth to wherever it pleased her to go, she left one man on this poor earth in a state of aloneness and loss as he has never known, an aloneness for which there is no solace.

And my father? Well, we never understood him. I

suspect, never will. Not I, not my sister, not my brother. He's our favorite conversation piece, always has been, even though he's long passed away. We can talk about him for days on end. But he's beyond us.

Maybe we can't fathom him because he was there from the beginning, like the sky, the air, the light. Maybe we were too busy growing up, and then after that too busy marrying and working and raising kids and cain. Familiarity turned him into an unfathomable mystery.

Here's what he was like—about my height, skinny like me—maybe a trifle skinnier, if that's possible, especially as he got older, bald, always on the go, with a sizeable nose and mischievous brown eyes.

That's what he looked like. Then there were his ways and his ways were insuperably, overwhelmingly, ineffably impossible—inscrutable, unreasonable, beyond comprehension, human or divine. You'd start to talk of something, simple talk, innocuous talk and in a trice you'd find yourself knee-deep in the wallows of an argument, being terribly misunderstood, with the past being raked up and cast in your face, with ghastly accusations flying. With him pronouncing, "You don't like to hear the truth! That's your problem!"

My father was very concerned about the truth, as all

fathers should be. This preoccupation with truth ran into everything and it was connected with his obsession with keeping things in order. Everything had a place. Socks didn't belong under a bed. The broom belonged in the corner by the chimney. The milk bottle had its particular spot in the refrigerator. Everything had a specific and proper place. He liked to fix things, too. Given world enough and time he could have straightened out the Leaning Tower of Pisa. He could fix ballpoint pens, he could fix radios, bicycles, washing machines, televisions. Before he would yield anything to the rubble heap he would work into the night, puttering, wrenching, tinkering—never say die!

And that's another thing about him. He couldn't bear to have anything die. He'd try to save even one tiny drooping basil plant. He saw a use for everything, anything he came across, a present or potential use. That's why he saved all manner of things. Scraps of string, rubber bands, tinfoil—what other people throw away, he made huge balls of them. Pieces of wire, plastic bags. He would bend old bent nails back into shape. He moved over the earth like a beachcomber, salvaging whatever life flung up on the shore. He never believed in waste.

It doesn't sound so weird now that I'm writing about it, but way back then it used to drive us wild. The kitchen drawers were stuffed with paper bags and plastic bags and all-size rubber bands and Raleigh coupons and paper clips. In every corner of the house: coffee cans with odd things in them, twigs and walnut shells and such. There were fan belts hanging in the garage and bicycle wheels and parts of lamps, chair legs, curtain rods. And piles and piles of paper, paper of all types and sizes.

Paper was an important thing in our house because my father worked for a paper, a newspaper, *the* newspaper, the great *New York Daily News*, New York's Picture Newspaper. He worked nights, the lobster shift as it was called, for years and years, hard, assiduously, in season and out, sick or not. He wanted to work, hated to miss a day. When the time came to retire he did it resentfully. He was a hard-working man. He had a printing business on the side, too. When he had a day off he worked on the house.

He took care of things, and kept everything going. He took care of us, too, my mother and my sister and brother and I. We lacked for nothing. We were never even close to being well off but we had what we needed. He, my father, provided it all.

That's it! Impossible as he was or seemed, he gave us everything! That's what a father is supposed to do, isn't it? He's the giver. That's what the word, dad, means. He was the giver. He gave me everything, and he taught me everything.

He taught me how to catch and how to hit and how to run, how to ride a bicycle, how to eat, how to say thank you, how to work, how to clean up afterwards, how to take care of things, how to focus, how to pay attention to detail, how to get to the root of a problem and repair a thing, how to smile. He taught me to respect things. He taught me what to value. He taught me to live—while I was alive and had time on my side.

He taught me everything, by what he said but even more by what he did and the way he did it. Like the way he set type, which as an old-time compositor, he did by hand. He had a printing press downstairs in the basement and on weekends he would do wedding invitations and business cards. I'd watch him for hours, his fingers flashing in and out of tiny compartments in an immense, shallow drawer, unerringly plucking out the tiny metal letters and creating words with them and out of the words creating sentences. A magical process. Then he'd bind all the words together, lock it up tight and put it into the press, ink the rollers and start the great rumbling machine going, and the sound of it went all through the house. The press would open and close like an alligator's jaws and my father would feed it blank cards or papers and then he would reach in, unintimidated, and deftly pull out the printed copy. He never missed.

Funny how everything I'm doing now is what he used to do, only in a different way—even to his persistent straining for perfection. I look at my hands and I see my father's hands. I hear myself laugh and I hear my father's laugh. The older I get the more I get like him.

I think I'm beginning to understand him, now. What made it so difficult when he was alive, through all those long years, before he got that stroke—alone—looking for a tool in the cellar, was that we, my brother and sister and I, we never realized that he was a person, a real person, long before he became our father. And now that we're all out on our own, as we say, he continues, wherever he may be, he continues on in his own incomparable way—a person.

There's one more picture of him that comes into my mind. It's one that keeps coming back. It's of him, my father, at Coney Island, swimming. He was at home in the water. High waves, low waves, shallow water, deep. I remember him going out farther and farther, past everyone else, past earshot, out, out into the deep water. He moved easily, gracefully, with long, strong strokes, as if he was dreaming his way out there. He was imperturbable, confident in his powers, trustful, with no doubt in the willingness of the great ocean to uphold him.

We—I—watching on the shore wondered and admired him. I worried some, but I was confident in him. I was proud of his daring. He was my father and he was out there by himself. Alone, unafraid, meeting himself.

Well, there you are, Mom and Dad. Bless you both. I will love you and honor you till my last breath.

About Our Author

Frank Crocitto has the distinction of having been an actor, a milkman, a salesman, a garbage collector, a house painter, a janitor, a farmer, an attendant in a mental hospital, a teacher of Gymnastics, Mathematics, English, Theater and even Insight—and now—a writer. But distinctions don't give the gist of a man, though they give indications of where he's been, what he's done, and—if he's been looking—what he has seen.

One thing Frank has seen is Brooklyn. Born 7-7-1937 in Staten Island—before it was colonized by the civilized isle of Manahatta—he soon enough took root in Brooklyn's Dyker Heights, where he discovered the possibilities of a spaldeen, the joys of stickball and the wisdom of the streets. Ask him now where he "learned to be such a wise guy," and he'll tell you it was "on the block," the block being 81st Street between 13th and 14th Avenue.

He also gleaned some of his smarts from his studies, which took place at P.S. 201, New Utrecht High, and Brooklyn College. He has, in fact, been described as a zealous scholar, and he's focused his scholastic attention on the best humankind has to offer. His deep appreciation of the great American Transcendentalists—Henry David Thoreau, Ralph Waldo Emerson and Walt Whitman—led to a collaboration with vision-impaired photographer John Dugdale on the book *New Suns Will Arise*, extracting sublime lines from Thoreau's journals to illuminate Dugdale's cyanotype portraits. He leapt whole-heartedly into the poetry of Gerard Manly Hopkins, learned to recite it, and wrote a radio-play for the *Ave Maria Hour* based on Hopkin's tragic end, entitled *The Handsome Heart*. And his embracing of the writings of Stephen Crane has produced several stage plays based on Crane's short stories. Frank's rendering of *The Bride Comes To Yellow Sky* has been performed all over the United States for over thirty years.

You can learn a lot about the man by what he keeps in his filing cabinet. Actually, he has eight of them, in various states of "sortedness," which periodically produce new projects to work on when he's supposed to be cleaning out the files. A novel, *The Gravesend Crucifiers*—reams of plays, including his rendition of an unfinished Oscar Wilde work, and a romance set in Civil War times— jaunty love poems filled with a lust for language—a vast collection of esoteric lore that serves as centerpoint for the short blasts of illumination in his monthly column, *Frankly Speaking*—a book about Jesus, his hero—the makings of a children's book detailing the underground adventures of three potatoes.

For all of his far-reaching interests, Frank's focus of late has been Brooklyn—mythologized not only in *A Child's Christmas* but also a collection of short stories, *Insight is Better than Ice Cream*. These parables of the sweet Brooklyn streets of his boyhood—his school days—his first job—his first dog—and his first (and last) Midnight Green Cadillac have opened up a world where stickball reigns supreme and there's a lesson to be learned on every streetcorner.

There's more about Frank, of course, but you can't talk about Frank without talking about his dog, and he usually won't pass up a chance to drop a dog story on you if you're game. Sparkplug's the name (of the dog, that is) and for every serious endeavor Frank the thinker embarks on, he always brings an element of pure dog-gedness to the situation—Sparky doesn't let him forget about the basics. Frank has a deep sense of the connection between man and dog, and has even promised a book of dog stories before long.

There's also the literary rhapsody in praise of man's (and woman's) favorite topic, *Hooray for Love*. Frank makes it his business to love his dogs, but he loves his wife Betty like nobody's business. When he reads aloud one of the poems from *Hooray*, which depicts a simple scene of Betty with their grandson, his voice floods with love, and wavers a bit, as if tickled with salt water.

And all of this shoveling through past snows of Brooklyn has inspired further developments in the *Child's Christmas* saga—a novel. Look for the unabridged, unexpurgated, unrelenting version of *A Child's Christmas in Brooklyn: The Novel* for next year's stocking stuffer (and get a big stocking).

Of course, there's nothing like meeting the man, but perhaps through his books you'll run into him—still swinging—down on the eternal 81st.

—The Publisher

Complete your Crocitto Collection—

order Frank's books from Candlepower and get your copy
PERSONALLY INSCRIBED AND AUTOGRAPHED

Vincent Anastasio / Harvey Garrett

Frank with his ghost-writer, Sparkplug

INSIGHT IS BETTER THAN ICE CREAM

A CHILD'S CHRISTMAS IN BROOKLYN

HOORAY FOR LOVE

THE SECRET MEANING OF CHRISTMAS

NEW SUNS WILL ARISE

ALL TITLES AVAILABLE FROM

CANDLEPOWER

WWW.CANDLEPOWER.ORG

FRANK CROCITTO

INSIGHT

IS
BETTER
THAN
ICE CREAM

A COLLECTION OF THEMES FOR
RE-COLLECTING YOUR SELF

Insight is Better than Ice Cream

Read Insight once, it's funny, poignant, inspiring.
Read it again—there's something serious going on
beneath that sly Brooklyn patter.
Then read it out loud, and listen as
the pages become parable.
And not just your same-old,
run-of-the-mill parables.
These really happened.

"Great Storytelling with Gems of Wisdom. One of the best books of practical philosophy I have encountered. Frank Crocitto tells his own stories of seeking and finding. They are as funny as they are deep, full of amusing anecdotes and hard-earned insights." ✱✱✱✱✱Five Stars

—Amazon.com

FRANK CROCITTO

HOORAY

LOVE

a lyrical journey to the source

Hooray for Love

Frank Crocitto and designer David Perry have woven
poetry, prose, drama and essays around the evocative
image-themes from Botticelli's *La Primavera*,
one of the Italian Master's finest paintings.
The result is *Hooray for Love*, which features
the hilarious springtime-in-New York vignette
"May I in the Merry Merry,"
and the practical tale of a search for True Love,
"Hooray for Love."

> *"...begins with a laugh and ends with a call to action. Working the room with the eloquence of a Shakespearean suitor, the sly cunning of a confidence man, and the fervor of an old-time tent revivalist, Crocitto leads the reader on a tour of the many types and guises of love, lulling the reader with sweet words awakening them to unexpected possibilities.*
>
> *...a book modeled on experience, written with wit, and aiming toward the triumph of love."*
>
> —*Brian K. Mahoney, editor, Chronogram magazine*

A Child's Christmas in Brooklyn

The Audio Book

Available on cassette or compact disc.

A boy in Brooklyn in the 40's.

A loving family and its holiday hurly-burly.

The universal mystery of Santa Claus—solved.

You've read the Christmas classic by Frank Crocitto. Now you can hear the story voiced by the author himself. With touches of musical delight from composer Eric Wilson.

HERE'S HOW TO ORDER

INSIGHT IS BETTER THAN ICE CREAM
SOFTCOVER BOOK $14.95
A CHILD'S CHRISTMAS IN BROOKLYN
HARDCOVER BOOK $14.95
A CHILD'S CHRISTMAS IN BROOKLYN: THE AUDIO
CASSETTE OR COMPACT DISC $15.95
HOORAY FOR LOVE
HARDCOVER BOOK $16.95
THE SECRET MEANING OF CHRISTMAS
PAMPHLET $4.95

ALSO AVAILABLE FROM CANDLEPOWER:
NEW SUNS WILL ARISE
HARDCOVER BOOK
PUBLISHED BY HYPERION $24.95

GO TO OUR WEBSITE
WWW.CANDLEPOWER.ORG

CALL US TOLL - FREE
1- 888 - 744 -1317

OR WRITE TO US
ORDERS@CANDLEPOWER.ORG
CANDLEPOWER
P.O. BOX 787
NEW PALTZ, NY 12561